My Book about Life in Jesus' Time

by Robert Baden
Illustrated by Michelle Dorenkamp

SAINT LOUIS

Library of Congress Cataloging-in-Publication Data

Baden, Robert, 1936-
    My book about life in Jesus' time / Robert Baden.
       p.   cm.
    ISBN 0-570-05036-7
    1. Sociology, Biblical—Juvenile literature. 2. Bible. N.T. Gospels—Social scientif-
ic criticism—Juvenile literature. 3. Palestine—Social life and customs—To 70 A.D.—
Juvenile literature. 5. Jesus Christ—Childhood—Juvenile literature. I. Title.
BS2555.6.S55B33   1998
225.9'5—dc21
                                        97-27909
                                          AC

1 2 3 4 5 6 7 8 9 10   07 06 05 04 03 02 01 00 99 98

Contents

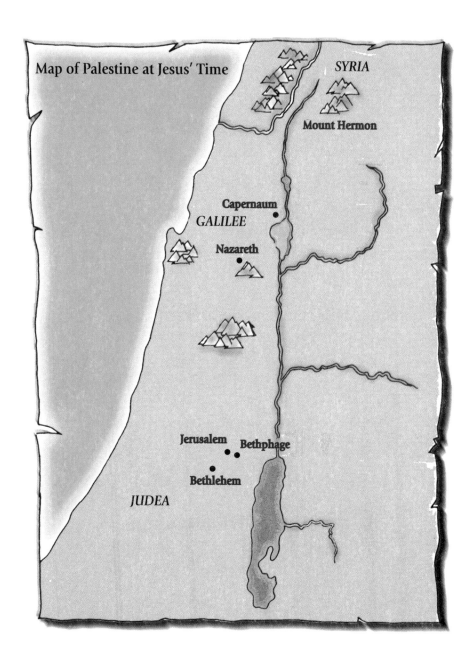

Map of Palestine at Jesus' Time

SYRIA

Mount Hermon

Capernaum

GALILEE

Nazareth

Jerusalem Bethphage

Bethlehem

JUDEA

The World when Jesus Lived

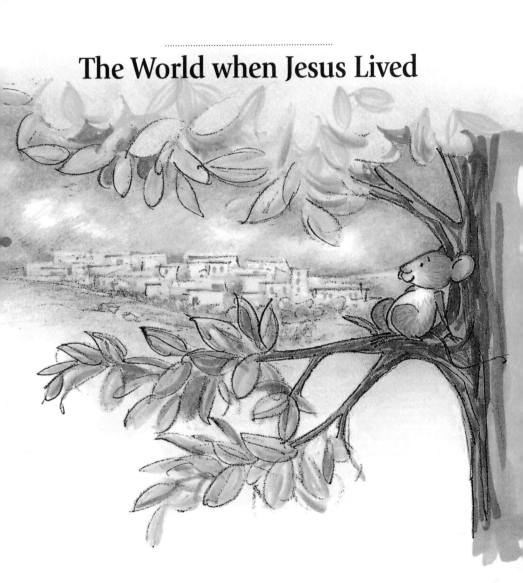

You know that Jesus Christ was born
Two thousand years ago;
And how He died and rose again,
You surely also know.

You know how much He loves us all
And how He answers prayer,
But where He lived, you might not know,
Or the things that He did there.

This book shows plants and animals
That lived where Jesus walked.
You'll learn of weddings in His day
And the languages He talked.

The things you learn here may seem
        strange,
Like anything that's new,
But they will teach you something more
About our Savior too.

Jesus lived in Palestine,
A country by the sea.
Though born down south in Bethlehem,
He grew up in Galilee.

This country wasn't very large,
Much like a smaller state.
One hundred fifty miles in length
Is really not that great.

The weather there was hot and dry;
It almost never snowed.
And strong winds blew all summer long
Down every dusty road.

In wintertime, the rains would come,
Sometimes enough to flood.
This needed rainfall filled the wells
But turned the roads to mud.

Trees greened, and flowers appeared in
    spring:
Cypress, olive, fig,
Pomegranates, roses, grapes—
Plants both small and big.

Many different kinds of birds
Soared through the skies above:
Eagles, ravens, vultures, hawks,
Quail, storks, and doves.

Animals were often used
By people Jesus knew:
Donkeys, camels, oxen, mules,
Sheep and cattle too.

Creatures roamed outside the towns:
Leopards, snakes, and frogs;
Badgers, porcupines, and deer;
Scorpions, wild dogs.

Cats and dogs were common too,
But not as pets to keep.
Cats were evil, people thought,
And dogs killed hens and sheep.

When a boy was at the marriage age,
His parents picked his mate.
Engagements often were arranged
Without a single date!

Most girls got married very young,
(Fourteen was quite respected).
The boys they married had no choice;
They took the girl selected.

For days inside the bride's own home
The wedding feast took place.
Eating, laughter, song, and dance
Filled each and every space.

These people used more languages
Than most of us can speak:
Aramaic every day,
Hebrew, too, and Greek.

Since Rome had conquered Palestine,
Most knew some Latin too.
But freedom from this Roman rule
Was the hope of every Jew.

For sixty years the power of Rome
Had enforced the Roman law,
And Roman soldiers cruel and proud
Were the only ones folks saw.

The people didn't get to vote;
Their taxes were unfair.
For Jewish customs and our God,
The Romans had no care.

In spite of Roman rule, the Jews
Still had their holy days,
Those special times they set aside
To celebrate and praise.

Like Hanukkah or "Feast of Lights,"
The Tabernacle Feast,
Purim's Feast, Atonement Day,
Rosh Hashanah not the least.

Passover, though, was chief of all,
Remembering the way
That God spared Israel's firstborn sons
When Egypt's died that day.

Homes and Towns when Jesus Lived

Most houses built in Jesus' day
Were usually quite small.
They only had a single room
And were just one story tall.

This room was used for everything—
To work, sleep, eat, or play.
There babies came and people died;
There worshipers would pray.

The roof was flat; on summer days
The people chose to cook there.
And also on hot summer nights
Their beds they often took there.

They slept on mats, so making beds
Was not a problem for them.
At night they rolled mats out; at dawn
They rolled them up again.

The homes were built of stone or bricks
Made from mud or clay.
There were no windowpanes or doors—
Imagine that today!

The open space was hung with cloth
Or covered up with skin.
These couldn't keep the animals
Or cold from coming in.

The floors were only dirt or stones—
Impossible to clean.
The kind of house we have today
Was never ever seen.

The women swept the floors with sand,
Which soaked up grease that fell.
They also cleaned their plates with sand,
But it didn't work too well.

Homes had no electric lights;
There were no candles yet.
Light came from bowls of oil in which
A burning wick was set.

Today we turn a faucet on
And out comes lots of water.
In Jesus' day, it came from wells,
Brought home by wife or daughter.

A bath or shower every day
Would never have been seen.
Ashes, oil, perfume were used
In an effort to keep clean.

Most towns back then, like Nazareth,
Were really very small.
Fifty homes or less, some stores,
A worship place—that's all.

And even great Jerusalem
Was no city like today.
Forty thousand at the most
Lived there in Jesus' day.

Strong walls surrounded larger towns;
Each wall contained a gate.
These towns were safe from enemies
That came there filled with hate.

Travel back in Jesus' day
Was not by plane or car.
Since people walked on rocky paths,
They seldom traveled far.

And traveling from town to town
Alone was filled with danger.
Robbers hid along the way;
No one could trust a stranger.

Every year all people tried—
Although it wasn't simple—
To travel to Jerusalem
To worship in the temple.

That temple in Jerusalem
Stood high above the city.
Of marble, gold, and precious woods,
It certainly looked pretty.

But people usually stayed at home,
Waiting ages long,
For a Savior who would come
To change all that was wrong.

Food and Clothing when Jesus Lived

We've got McDonald's and Pizza Hut
Where we get food to please us,
But eating places such as these
Were never known by Jesus.

He never sampled Chinese food;
No ice-cream stores were handy.
He had no hamburgers or pop,
No lemonade or candy.

Yet food and eating were a major
Part of Jewish life.
For meals were a family time
For husband, children, wife.

The oven used for heat was often
Used for cooking too.
The food cooked there or cooked outside
Was much like barbecue.

The food was placed upon the floor;
The family took a seat.
The father blessed the food, and then
They all began to eat.

The most important food was bread.
Their other menu varied:
Melons, dates, dried fish, or lamb;
Plant roots, figs, or berries.

They used no knives or forks or spoons;
They ate their food by hand.
Some children even now might think
This way to eat was grand.

Their drinks were water, wine, or milk,
And sometimes tea was brewed.
Honey was a special treat,
And sugar cane was chewed.

The clothing worn told much about
The people of the time.
Dark colors said that they were sad;
Bright colors said, "I'm fine!"

A rich man wore a robe of silk;
A poor one's clothes were tattered.
And where a person came from was
Another thing that mattered.

Most people, men and women, wore
Loose, flowing robes a lot.
These kept them cooler in a land
Where summers were so hot.

Unmarried women could not wear
What married women wore.
And women weren't allowed to go
Beyond the temple door.

And in the temple men were told
Their heads must not be bare.
They wore a prayer shawl, a tallith,
Whenever they went there.

To cover up their feet, most wore
Crude sandals made of skin,
But at a house they took them off
Before they entered in.

When people needed clothes or food
They couldn't make or grow,
The busy, noisy marketplace
Was the place that they would go.

There sellers sold fresh vegetables,
Spices, fish, or wood;
Leather, silk, perfume, and jewels—
They sold all that they could.

The people often traded goods
To get the things they needed.
A chicken for a water jug—
Most often this succeeded.

Coins also could be used to buy
Whenever folks could get them.
Shekels, drachmas, "mites" were used,
Or jewels if sellers let them.

The people had no radios
Or TVs they could use,
So many times they also came
To the marketplace for news.

Schools and Churches
when Jesus Lived

The schools when Jesus lived were not
Like schools we have today.
Just boys, not girls, could go, and they
Had little time to play.

These students had no books to read,
So their teachers talked instead.
Each boy would listen closely and
Remember what was said.

The teachers were called "rabbis" then.
They told their nation's story,
Of Adam, Joseph, kings, and wars:
The days of Israel's glory.

They heard of Noah and the flood,
Of Abraham and Saul,
Of Moses and the Exodus—
They learned about them all.

They learned about the history
Of their people since creation.
They also learned that God would send
A Savior to His nation.

Not all of education, though,
Took place inside the schools.
At home both boys and girls learned how
To work and follow rules.

At home their mothers taught young girls
The skills they'd need to marry.
They learned to cook, make clothes, clean
     house,
How best large loads to carry.

When school was out, their fathers taught
The boys a skill or craft.
If girls did more than cook and sew,
People might have laughed.

Some boys made pots, wove rugs, baked
    bread;
Some fished or learned to sing.
Some herded sheep, made wine or rope,
Or planted in the spring.

Young boys who learned to read and write
Took more respected roles:
Doctors, lawyers, rabbis, priests;
Wrote music, copied scrolls.

But children still had time for fun,
For games and wild chases;
For ring-toss, hide-and-seek, and dolls;
For marbles, tag, and races.

Like schools, the church when Jesus lived
Was different from today.
The thing we'd notice first was this:
It met on Saturday.

Way back when God first made the world,
He took a day to rest.
All Jewish people since that day
Treat the Sabbath Day as blessed.

At sunset every Friday night
Their worship time began.
Candles, prayers, stories, food—
All followed the same plan.

No one worked at all on Saturday.
They worshiped God instead.
They went to church, their *synagogue,*
As God's own Word had said.

The priests there spoke God's holy Word;
The people sang and prayed.
They heard the stories of the past,
The promises God made.

Most Christians don't use Saturday
As their "church day" any longer.
Jesus rose on Sunday—that makes
The choice of that day stronger.

These foods and clothes, this kind of life,
Seem strange to us today.
But back in Jesus' day or now,
We're all alike in one way.

We sin each day, but Jesus died
And rose to set us free.
God loved this world so much that He
Did this for you and me.